North East Life
in the 1970s

by Andrew Clark & Sharyn Taylor

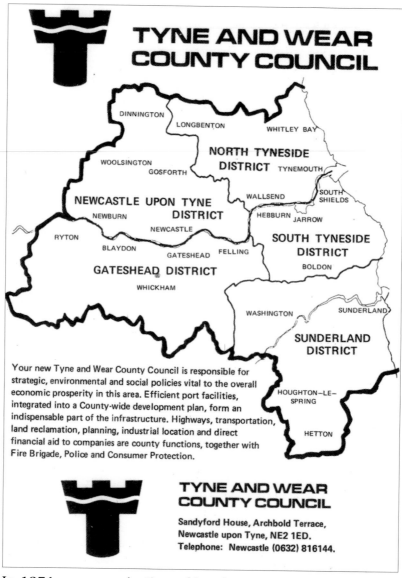

TYNE AND WEAR COUNTY COUNCIL

Your new Tyne and Wear County Council is responsible for strategic, environmental and social policies vital to the overall economic prosperity in this area. Efficient port facilities, integrated into a County-wide development plan, form an indispensable part of the infrastructure. Highways, transportation, land reclamation, planning, industrial location and direct financial aid to companies are county functions, together with Fire Brigade, Police and Consumer Protection.

TYNE AND WEAR COUNTY COUNCIL

Sandyford House, Archbold Terrace, Newcastle upon Tyne, NE2 1ED. Telephone: Newcastle (0632) 816144.

In 1974 a re-organisation of local government in England and Wales took place. This had a major impact in the North East where the Metropolitan County of Tyne and Wear was created. The county was only to last twelve years but in 2017 there are still a number of services that still operate across Tyne and Wear such as Fire & Rescue and Archives & Museums.

Copyright Andrew Clark & Sharyn Taylor 2017

First published in 2017 by

Summerhill Books
PO Box 1210, Newcastle-upon-Tyne NE99 4AH

www.summerhillbooks.co.uk

email: summerhillbooks@yahoo.co.uk

ISBN: 978-1-911385-18-9

Contents

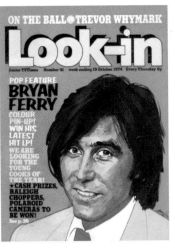

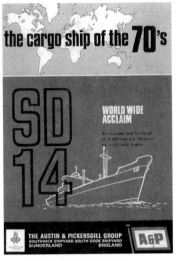

A view of the Consett Iron Works in the late 1970s. At this time heavy industry dominated the North East with coal mines, shipyards, glass works and engineering factories employing tens of thousands of people.

Acknowledgements

The authors would like to thank the following who have kindly helped with this book:

Alan Brett, John Carlson, Harry & Pauline Clark, Philip Curtis, Jim Harland, Tom Hutchinson, Mike Ingoe, George Nairn, Colin Orr, Mary Taylor and Neil Taylor.

The Chronicle, The Journal, Sunderland Echo, Evening Gazette
Gateshead Library, Newcastle Library
West Newcastle Picture History Collection
Alamy

Bibliography

Ashington Coal Company – The Five Collieries by Mike Kirkup, The People's History
Benwell, Buses & Boxing – The Story of Audrey Guthrie by Andrew Clark, Summerhill Books
Ellington Colliery Through The Years by Neil Taylor, Summerhill Books
Mike Hodges by Mark Adams, Pocket Essentials
Saltwell Park – The Story of the People's Park by Anthea Lang, Summerhill Books
Shildon & District by Tom Hutchinson, The People's History
The Clubs of Gateshead by Peter Annable, Summerhill Books
The Kindness of Strangers by Kate Adie, Headline Book Publishing

Introduction

The 1970s was an interesting decade in the North East. Perhaps it is not as memorable as the 'Swinging Sixties' but there was still lots going on in our region. We, the authors of this book, were children in the '70s and so this is reflected in the memories we have of Christmas, holidays, games, toys, music, films and television.

The book features many events, people and stories from the 1970s. One day many people remember was Decimal Day when the old pounds, shillings and pence were replaced by a hundred pennies to the pound. The fashions of the day are featured such as flared trousers, satin blouses, double denim and leatherwear. The music scene of the 1970s was very vibrant with North East artists such as Geordie, Lindisfarne, Alan Price, Bryan Ferry and Sting. On television people enjoyed *Whatever Happened to The Likely Lads*, *When The Boat Comes In* and *The Paper Lads* for younger viewers. While on the big screen the iconic film *Get Carter* starring Michael Caine is a vivid portrait of Tyneside in the early '70s. The region's industrial past is recalled with shipbuilding on the Tyne and Wear, mining memories as well as the industrial action that led to the 'Winter of Discontent' and power cuts. There were also the memorable cup runs of our football teams – Sunderland, Newcastle and Blyth Spartans.

Two models pose in '70s fashions in the grounds of Gosforth Park Hotel.

This book is not a complete history of the 1970s in the North East but does give a snapshot of what life was like during the decade. If any readers have any interesting stories they would like to share we would be happy to hear from you. Please email us at:

summerhillbooks@yahoo.co.uk

Andrew Clark & Sharyn Taylor

A view of the High Level Bridge and the Swing Bridge looking towards Newcastle from the Gateshead side in the 1970s.

A 1970s Childhood
by Andrew Clark

I was born in 1967 so my memories of the 1970s are childhood ones. To me, thinking about those days, summers seemed to be hotter and winters were colder. Perhaps I'm just remembering the heat wave of 1976 and the bad winter of 1978/79.

My childhood was very different from youngsters today. There were no mobile phones, computers or kindles and our latest electronic gadgets were things like Big Trak, Simon or Speak & Spell. However, in the '70s people like Steve Jobs of Apple and Bill Gates of Microsoft were starting to work on the technology that would in later decades change all of our lives.

SOUTHFIELD GREEN, Cramlington

This attractive 4-bedroomed semi detached house is the H48 at Southfield Green, £5,700 including garage and automatic gas fired central heating. An extensive range of homes includes the H51, a 3-bedroomed semi detached house from £4,375; the T15, a 2-bedroomed terrace house from £3,600; the T37, a 3-bedroomed terrace house from £3,990 and the F31 a superb 2-bedroomed flat from £3,150. All including selective duct air heating.

Bell homes carry a six months free maintenance guarantee plus a 10 year guarantee as members of the N.H.B.R.C.

Mortgages freely available.

So Roomy!

Further information from:

John T Bell

At least books are as popular today as they were forty years ago. My first book was the one on the right – A Ladybird Easy-Reading Book: *People at Work The Sailor*. It was first published the year I was born.

My parents bought their first house in Cramlington in 1976 for £11,000 and it was similar to the one advertised on the left from 1971. One of the selling points was the 'duct air heating' that a lot of homes had. I used to send my toy soldiers on 'missions' into these ducts and some never came back. We got our first house phone when we moved to Cramlington and it was one of those wonderful 'trim' phones (*left*) that were very popular at the time. Before that we had to use a street telephone box to make calls.

Below are some of my favourites from the decade. How many do readers remember and what are your favourites from the 1970s?

A LADYBIRD EASY-READING BOOK
People at Work
THE SAILOR

1970s Favourites

Favourite TV programmes
Doctor Who, Starsky and Hutch, Six Million Dollar Man

Favourite Films
Star Wars, Superman, The Land That Time Forgot

Favourite Toys
Action Man, Airfix Models, Frustration

Favourite Sweets
Midget Gems, Ten pence mix-ups

First Holiday
Butlins at Filey in 1973 (*right*)

Sliding down the helter-skelter at Filey,

These are my favourites as a child and some have changed since then. My favourite films of the '70s are now the Godfather, the French Connection and Apocalypse Now.

Andrew Clark

A 1970s Baby
by Sharyn Taylor

I was born in South Shields in 1975. My Dad worked away a lot when I was a child and the photograph on the right shows him working on an oil rig. Lots of dads had to work away in the 1970s as the shipyards and factories were closing in the North East. Whole families would move to the midlands or the south as parents looked for new jobs.

Dad told me years later that when he first went on the oil rigs in the early '70s that he thought the safety conditions were dreadful.

My Mam had full-time job looking after me and my younger sister and brother. We would spend summer days at the beach in South Shields (see page 20) and our Christmas presents were bought from Binns. There's a photograph of us three kids with Santa at Binns in South

My favourite TV programme when I was little was *Bagpuss*. It was first shown in 1974 and was the story of an old cat and lots of other toys.

Shields on page 30. One of the earliest toys I can remember getting for Christmas is the cuddly monkey that is shown on the left. I still treasure this monkey which has a zip at the back to put your pyjamas in.

We had lots of animals at home when we were young – two Chow Chow dogs, rabbits, and geese at the bottom of the garden and, before I was born, Dad even had a real monkey!

1970s Favourites

Favourite TV programmes
Bagpuss, Magic Roundabout, Wacky Races

Favourite Films
Black Beauty, Watership Down

Favourite Toys
Cuddly toys –
Womble, monkey and bunny rabbit (*right*)

Favourite Sweets
Dolly Mixtures, Sherbet Fountain, Milkybar

First Holiday
Morecambe in 1975

Christmas Day and one of my presents, my bunny rabbit, is as big as me.

As I got older my favourite film from the 1970s is now Love Story with Ryan O'Neal and Ali MacGraw but I still enjoy watching Black Beauty and Watership Down as they are timeless classics.

Sharyn Taylor

Snapshots of the 1970s

Three lads peer into a derelict house in Mary Street, Silksworth, near Sunderland in the early 1970s. These former colliery houses had been built for miners working at Silksworth Colliery around 1900 and at that time they were comfortable homes for families, however, sixty years later they were hardly suitable for modern needs. The late 1960s and early '70s saw a radical change in housing in the North East. Many streets of terraced houses or flats, where sometimes families lived in poor conditions, were demolished. People were moved to new estates often on the outskirts of town or to high rise tower blocks. As the old houses were demolished they became playgrounds for youngsters like the photograph above shows.

Left: One of the many terraced streets in Byker, Newcastle, around 1970. In the 1970s, streets like this were swept away to be replaced by new housing and the Byker Wall.

Below: An artist's impression of how new housing would look in Byker in the 1970s. The most famous part of the development was the Byker Wall but hundreds of houses and flats were also built to the south of the wall.

A booklet produced by Newcastle City Council in 1969 gave this description of the proposed Byker redevelopment:

'The City Council are aiming to provide a more attractive environment than that achieved on some new housing estates. Ralph Erskine (the architect) is proposing materials like brown brick and timber, brightly coloured wooden fences, and other timber work to make new housing areas look attractive and lively. The structure of the houses is being kept simple and economical, so that as much money as possible can be spent inside, on the layout of kitchens and other rooms, where the housewife gets the benefit.'

This 1971 advert from Courtelle calls Spennymoor 'the fashion-leader'. The company produced knitwear at its County Durham factory in the 1970s.

An advert for the Moti Mahal Restaurant, Newcastle from 1970 – 'the first Tandoori Indian Restaurant in the North.' The following year it is said that one of Britain's favourite dishes – Chicken Tikka Masala – was invented in an Indian restaurant in Glasgow.

Right: A promotion for the 'Hillman Imp De Luxe' at the Gosforth Park Hotel, around 1970. At this time you could buy a brand new Ford Escort for £820, a Cortina for £950, a Mini for £640 and VW Beetle for around £980.

A very fashionable apprentice from Swan Hunter's Haverton Hill shipyard talks to the Duchess of Kent in 1970. The Duchess was at the yard to launch the *Furness Bridge*. Ships were built at Haverton Hill on the Tees for nearly sixty years before the yard closed in 1979.

Benwell in Newcastle in the 1970s. In the background is a flat-roofed shopping centre with Paul's Boutique on the far right. Like a number of shopping centres built in the late 1960s and early '70s it was demolished within a couple of decades.

Bourgogne's pub in Newgate Street in Newcastle around 1970. This ancient pub was formerly the Mason's Arms dating from the mid 1600s. In the late 19th century it was taken over by a French winemaker and merchant. The pub was refurbished and renamed Bourgogne's. All of this history was swept away when the pub and this part of Newgate Street was demolished in the early '70s as the city centre was redeveloped. As old pubs were being pulled down in the 1970s, new ones in Newcastle, such as the Nelson in Walker (*below*), were being built. Whereas Bourgogne's survived centuries, the Nelson, like many 1970s buildings was open only decades before it was closed and demolished.

Left: An advert for new flats and town houses in Jesmond Park East, near to Jesmond Dene, in Newcastle from 1971. The flats in Dene Court are being offered at £7,750 while the three-storey town houses were £9,750. In 2016 a flat in Dene Court was for sale at £165,000 while one of the town houses was priced at £320,000.

This distinctive building in Gateshead used to be the Boilermakers' Social Club in Charles Street. It was built in 1969 in a shape resembling a boiler. In 1978 the club was bought by the comedian Bobby Patterson and renamed 'The Talk of the Tyne'. In the following decades it became a disco, a church, a council building and then was knocked down.

The heyday of the juvenile jazz bands was the 1960s but they were still popular in the early to mid 1970s. Here are the New Silksworth Skyliners Jazz Band who were formed in 1962. They must have been a successful band as they have dozens of cups and trophies. A local jazz band was featured in the film *Get Carter* – the Pelaw Hussars.

Right: A sign for Tudor Crisps on sale in a shop in Tynemouth in the early 1970s. Tudor was a very popular make of crisps that were originally made  in Newcastle before the firm moved to a factory in Peterlee. At that time there were three main brands in Britain – Tudor, Smiths and Walkers. Eventually, Walkers came to dominate the crisps market in the UK, helped by a series of adverts by Gary Lineker. Walkers dominance saw the Tudor brand disappear and Smiths reducing their products to just the most popular snacks. Tudor are remembered with fondness in the North East for their popular, and sometimes unusual flavours; special offers such as 'Wear-em Scare-ems' medallions (*above right*); and TV adverts. Their most memorable advert was the one where the paper boy offers his friend 'A canny bag of Tudor' if he finishes off his round. The answer: 'For Tudor I'll climb a mountain' – and a mountain it is as the papers have to be delivered to a tower block in Dunston where the lift is not working.

In the early '70s the Woolco stores in Killingworth (*above*) and Washington (*right*) were a new form of shopping – the superstore. The Washington Woolco was opened by Pat Phoenix – Coronation Street's Elsie Tanner – in 1973. The stores were part of the Woolworth's group but the superstores were not a success and most were closed or sold in the 1980s.

Woolco shopping is coming to Washington

WOOLCO
DEPARTMENT STORE
WASHINGTON NEW TOWN CENTRE

Grand Opening Wednesday May 30th
BY PATRICIA PHOENIX
(Elsie Howard of Granada T.V.'s Coronation Street)

Decimalisation

On 15th February 1971 a radical change took place in Britain when the old system of pounds, shillings and pence (known as £sd with 12 pennies in a shilling and 20 shillings in a pound) was replaced with the decimal currency of a hundred pennies in a pound. That date in February became known as D Day – Decimal Day.

Right: One of the booklets issued by the Decimal Currency Board who managed the transition. Two weeks before D Day the Board issued these instructions to the public:

- The £ stays the same but is made up of 100 new pence.
- There will be £sd shops and decimal shops.
- Decimal shops will charge £p prices and give the new 'coppers' in change.
- £sd will trade as now.
- You can use both old and new coins in either kind of shop.
- If in doubt, give more and get change.

In 1971 Harry Clark was working for the NHS as an auditor and one of his jobs in the run up to decimalisation was to go round local hospitals to inform staff of the changes. He said there were a lot of concerns about the new money:

'People were terrified in the run up to D Day and thought it would be a disaster. I had to go into offices where staff handled petty cash and show them how to convert the old pounds, shillings and pence into the new pence and pounds. When we started everyone thought it would be hard to work out and they would say 'I'll never get the hang of this' but when you think about it the new system was easier. All you had to remember was that there were a hundred pennies in a pound and just forget about shillings altogether. We had a chart with pictures of all the new coins on it that would soon be used and people did pick it up quite quickly. When D Day did come I can't remember anyone having any problems and people just got on with it.

'I'll never forget how worried people were and it was a bit like when they were talking about the 'Millennium Bug' in 1999. It was thought then that computers and other machines would stop working and that never happened.'

Despite all the worries before hand, D Day went very smoothly and one of the few complaints was that it was thought some shops took advantage of the change to raise their prices.

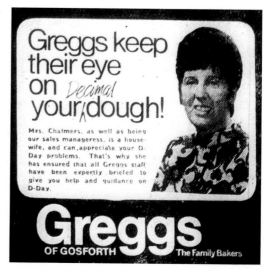

Left: An advert for Laws from 1971 with their food prices in old and new money. Corn flakes were 1 shilling 7d – 8 new pence.

Right: Greggs told customers they would 'keep their eye on your *decimal* dough' by briefing all their staff on D Day.

When the Lights Went Out

On 9th January 1972 the National Union of Mineworkers went on strike for an increase in their pay. The strike lasted until 25th February and some workers on the railways and the power stations joined the action by refusing to handle coal. This led to a shortage of fuel and measures were then brought in to reduce the use of electricity. By the middle of February there were power cuts for up to eight hours for many homes and businesses. Once the strike came to an end life returned to normal.

However, further industrial action by the miners two years later saw the country once again being plunged into darkness. The Conservative Government introduced a three day working week to restrict the use of electricity – hospitals and other essential services were exempt. Prime Minister Edward Heath called a General Election with the slogan 'Who governs Britain?'

Following the election, Labour's Harold Wilson became Prime Minister on 4th March 1974 and a few days later the miners' pay demands were met and the three day week came to an end. Over a quarter of a million miners accepted a 35% pay offer from the Labour Government which was double what the Conservatives were offering. This meant increases of between £6.71 and £16.31 on their weekly pay.

Right: An advert from February 1972 offering pensioners and others short of fuel the opportunity to keep warm at St Bede's Church hall, Town End Farm, Sunderland. People were told: 'Come and keep warm. Tell your neighbours.'

A cartoon from the *Sunderland Echo* looks at the funny side of how football could be played after the use of floodlights was banned in 1972.

The Three Day Week

Mike Coates recalls the days of the power cuts in the North East during the three day week of 1974:

"I was working for an insurance company in Jesmond during the power cuts. We had no lights on during the short winter days as well as no heating and we couldn't even boil a kettle to get hot drinks. The typists were allowed two candles, one on either side of their typewriters while the clerks had only one per desk. Candles were in short supply as was sugar for some reason. I remember spending lunch times walking round Newcastle city shops looking for both.

'At the time I lived in Cullercoats where we had a coal fire and an Aladdin paraffin fire for heating. I used to go to the local pub which had candles on the tables. We had to have bottled beer as the electric pumps were not working.

'We had friends who lived in North Shields next to Preston Hospital and sometimes we went there to watch television. As they were near the hospital they never had power cuts.'

A 'Flare' for Fashion

Right: A very fashionable Mary Taylor from South Shields around 1970. She is wearing a satin blouse with a black leather waistcoat and skirt. Mary recalls the fashions of the early '70s:

'I used to wear one-off items such as dresses which were made for me by Maurice Velody, a designer shop in Fowler Street, South Shields. I wore imitation mink coats, cowboy boots, wedged shoes as well as the satin blouse and leather waistcoat and skirt in the photograph.

'I also used to buy Simplicity patterns and cut the dress out and get clothes made by a dressmaker. I would buy two yards of material every week and have a new dress with a different colour every week.

'Broderie Anglaise was one of the main materials in the 1970s and it made a nice a-line dress. We used to dye our shoes the same colour as the dress we were wearing. I would put the shoes on the dustbin to dry.'

Left: Two photographs from a fashion show that was held at Gosforth Park Hotel in 1970. The models were employees of Newcastle Breweries and three of them pose in matching striped suits with flared trousers.

Right: An advert for Michael's – 'The Modern Man's Shop' – from 1972. At this time Michael's had branches on High Street West, Wallsend, Frederick Street, South Shields and Shields Road, Newcastle. Some of the items on sale were:

Afghan coats – £19.95

Flared trousers with turn ups – £4.25

Jacket, tulip lapel style, in Terylene Sarille (polyester) – £10.50

Three-piece suits, wide flared trousers with turn ups – £20.95

Fantastic range of superior suede and leather jackets – £15.50

Mod platform shoes and boots at keenest prices.

Football fashions – The crowd for Newcastle player Ollie Burton's testimonial against Sunderland at St James' Park in 1973. There is a mixture of woollen bobble hats, flat caps and headscarves worn by the fans. At the front a couple of Sunderland fans are in the middle of the United supporters.

Right: An advert for Chris B. Watson's fashion shop in South Shields from 1973. The references to 'Add that Final touch' and 'Just like Sunderland be in 'Top Gear' for the occasion' are because the Roker club had just reached the Cup Final at Wembley. Amongst the items on offer were:

Men's fashion shirts – £2.99

Flares from – £5.00

Oxford Bags – £6.60

Jackets made in the latest style from – £11.50

New in. The Denim Look Jackets from – £6.20

Sunderland fans on their way to an away game in 1978. At the front right, one fan has gone for the 'double denim' look with his waistcoat and turn up jeans. He completes his outfit with baseball boots.

Left: Kevin Keegan's fashionable look at Disneyland. In the 1970s Keegan was one of the biggest names in English football. After success at Liverpool he moved to Hamburg for £500,000 in 1977. While in Germany he was twice named European Footballer of the Year. A few years later he signed for Newcastle to become a Tyneside legend.

Mining Memories

Right: An advert from February 1971 to encourage men to consider mining as a career. The three men in the illustration appear to be at the match with their football scarves and rattle. Below the illustration are the words: 'Today, men get more from mining – a worthwhile job with good mates ...'

As well as offering a weekly basic wage of between £18 to £30, the National Coal Board were offering:

- Rates of pay among the highest in the region.
- Holidays – fortnight a year plus 13 days including public holidays all with pay.
- Concessionary fuel for all married households.
- Sick Pay Scheme.
- Housing available in some areas.
- No short time – guaranteed five days work.

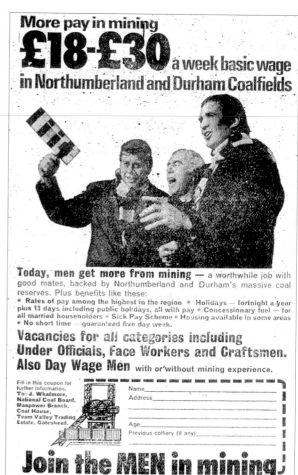

Left: Miners at Dawdon Colliery in Seaham come up from their shift in the 1970s. The advert above describes 'Northumberland and Durham's massive coal reserves' but pits like Dawdon were closed within twenty years.

A locomotive waits to transport a train of coal wagons from Wearmouth Colliery in Sunderland. Wearmouth was the last deep coal mine in the old county of Durham; surviving until 1993.

Above: Miners' parade through Ashington on 26th February 1972. The day before a seven week strike had been resolved that had started on 9th January. The miners' union had won a 21% pay increase for its members to make them the best paid industrial workers in the country. Before the strike they had been only seventeenth in the wage table. Included in the march above are men from the collieries of Ashington, Ellington, Lynemouth and Woodhorn. When Woodhorn Colliery was closed the site was turned into a museum.

Above: In the 1970s union leaders were household names because there was so much industrial strike action in the decade. There were none as well known as Joe Gormley, the President of the National Union of Mineworkers. Here he is talking to men at Ellington Colliery in 1976 when he was on a tour of the coalfields, campaigning support for miners' early retirement. Gormley was NUM President from 1971 to 1982 when he was succeeded by Arthur Scargill.

Left: In 1975 the combined pits of Ellington and Lynemouth produced over two million tons of coal in a year. At that time they were the world's biggest undersea mining operation.

The North East on Film

In 1971 the film *Get Carter* was released in cinemas. Michael Caine played the lead character in the tough thriller filmed in a number of locations in the North East.

Right: A poster for the movie which also starred Britt Ekland, Ian Hendry, George Sewell and Bryan Mosley. In one of the film's famous scenes Carter throws Mosley off the roof of the multi-storey car park in Gateshead town centre (*below*).

The film is based on the book *Jack's Return Home* by Ted Lewis. The novel is set in an un-named northern town. The only clues to its location is that Carter changes trains at Doncaster. There is also a reference to a letter received from Sunderland.

A number of towns and cities were considered for filming but it was director Mike Hodges who chose the region as the setting. He said: 'The key to *Get Carter* was finding a location that was hard … as soon as I saw Newcastle, with all these amazing steel bridges, rusty and brutal, I knew Jack Carter was home. And it was my kind of place. It was a working place, not a tourist attraction. It was a place where real people lived. This was where I wanted to make the film.'

Locations seen in the film include Gosforth Park Racecourse, the High Level Bridge, Frank Street in Benwell (with Dunston Power Station in the background), the Tyne Ferry and Blackhall Beach in East Durham (seen in the final shoot-out).

One of the scenes in *Get Carter* was filmed in the Victoria and Comet, Neville Street, Newcastle (*right*). After the cameras stopped rolling for the day the cast had a drink in the bar. When Michael Caine asked for half a lager the barman said that they didn't serve lager in the pub. When Caine asked why not the barman replied: 'We don't get many women in here.'

This was a time when lager and lime was a popular drink for ladies on a night out. As the decade progressed lager replaced beer as the 'usual' pint for a generation of lads.

In the 1979 advert (*above right*) Scottish and Newcastle were extolling the virtues of their traditional Exhibition Ale over that of lager.

An unusual scene in Alnwick Castle in August 1978 for the filming of the Walt Disney production *King Arthur and the Spaceman*. The film was based on the Mark Twain novel *A Connecticut Yankee in King Arthur's Court* and the cast included Kenneth More (King Arthur), Ron Moody (Merlin) and Jim Dale (Sir Mordred). The film was released under a number of different titles. One of them being *Unidentified Flying Oddball* – UFO.

Alnwick Castle has been used as a film location a number of times. For many it is most recognised as the setting for the wizard school of Harry Potter – Hogwarts.

One of the actors in *King Arthur and the Spaceman* was Rodney Bewes who is best known for his partnership with James Bolam in *The Likely Lads*. First made in black and white in the 1960s, the series returned ten years later in colour as *Whatever Happened to the Likely Lads*. Although the popular comedy was set in the North East, the 1960s series was mainly filmed in a studio. A bigger budget allowed the 1970s version to be filmed on location on Tyneside.

A number of successful sitcoms in that decade were made into films for the cinema. In 1976 *The Likely Lads* film (*right*) was released. The film included scenes in Newcastle, Wallsend, Whitley Bay and the Northumberland countryside.

Left: James Bolam, Rodney Bewes and Alun Armstrong in a scene from *The Likely Lads* film. Alun Armstrong, from Annfield Plain, County Durham, made his screen debut in *Get Carter*. Further film roles followed including: *A Bridge Too Far, Patriot Games, Braveheart, Sleepy Hollow* and *The Mummy Returns*. While filming *White Hunter Black Heart* he was surprised to see its star, Clint Eastwood, drink Newcastle Brown Ale on location.

Beside the Seaside

Happy Days at the Fair

The photograph above of me and Mam was taken at a photo booth at South Shields Fair (shown on the postcard above). In the days before we all had camera phones in our pocket, if you wanted to take a 'selfie' when you were out enjoying yourself then a photo booth would do. We lived in South Shields and we always spent the summer at the beach and the fair. On the back of my photo booth picture is written the date – 16th April 1976 – so I was just over a year old.

A few years later Mam took me and my younger sister and brother to the amusements. Mam had about £80 with her and us three kids managed to spend the lot! Most of it seemed to be spent on the machines that took 2 pences. At the end of the day we didn't have any money left – we didn't even have enough money for the bus fare home so we had to walk. Our house was at Cleadon Park which is on the outskirts of South Shields so it was a long walk home from the fair.

Sharyn Taylor

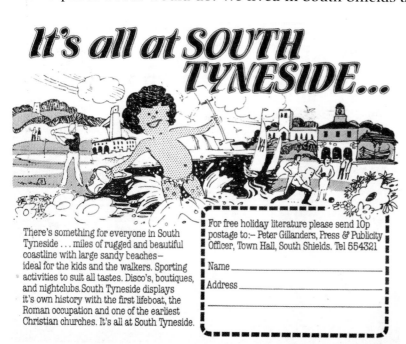

It's all at SOUTH TYNESIDE...

There's something for everyone in South Tyneside . . . miles of rugged and beautiful coastline with large sandy beaches – ideal for the kids and the walkers. Sporting activities to suit all tastes. Disco's, boutiques, and nightclubs. South Tyneside displays it's own history with the first lifeboat, the Roman occupation and one of the earliest Christian churches. It's all at South Tyneside.

For free holiday literature please send 10p postage to:– Peter Gillanders, Press & Publicity Officer, Town Hall, South Shields. Tel 554321

Name _____

Address _____

Above: An advert for the attractions of South Tyneside from the late 1970s. These included: 'miles of rugged and beautiful coastline with large sandy beaches – ideal for the kids and the walkers … South Tyneside displays its own history with the first lifeboat, the Roman occupation and one of the earliest Christian churches. It's all at South Tyneside.'

Right: A couple of youngsters enjoy a donkey ride on the beach at Seaton Carew, near Hartlepool, around 1970. Behind them can just be seen the concrete pillars of the shelter that was demolished in recent years. There are people making sandcastles and some beach tents at the far right.

A postcard of the North East's most famous seaside resort – Whitley Bay. Unusually, it does not include the famous landmark, the Spanish City. However, the postcard does show people enjoying plodgin' in the sea and strolling along the promenade as well as St Mary's Lighthouse that is still a popular spot today. After standing empty for many years, the Spanish City is now being developed for restaurants, shops and other leisure activities.

A snapshot of a bus at Seaburn around 1975 with the beach and sea in the background. Seaburn and Roker were advertised as 'Sunderland's Twin Resorts'.

The Big Dipper that was one of the many rides at Seaburn Fair. The resort had been built up in the 1930s and '50s and thousands would flock to it each summer. The Big Dipper was dismantled following a tragic fatality in 1972 and the gradual decline of the attractions at Seaburn continued as people went further afield for their holidays.

In recent years the word 'staycation' has become used as a term for those who spend their holidays near home. In this advert from 1970 'At Home Holidays' were being offered to 'see the beauty of the North at little expense, return to the comfort of your home each evening.'

Tours of the seaside, town or country were on offer from prices of £7 10 shillings or £8.

Where Ships Were Born

Right: The entrance to Swan Hunter's shipyard at Wallsend in 1973.

Former shipyard worker Peter Gibson recalls his time at Swan Hunter's in the 1970s:

'When I was twenty-one, and after serving my apprenticeship at JL Thompson's shipyard on the Wear, I left my employment there to seek a fresh challenge and to gain more experience in other yards. In April 1974 I began work as a shipwright at Swan Hunter's Wallsend shipyard.

'After showing my union card to the two shop stewards to prove that I was 'in benefit' I was sent to work with a shipwright called Ted who was a man in his fifties. Ted was a canny bloke who sort of took me under his wing, and on Fridays we used to go for a couple of pints during the dinner hour.

The launch of *Esso Hibernia* from Swan Hunter's in 1970.

Esso Hibernia being manoeuvred by tugs in the River Tyne after launch.

'We worked on the *Windsor Lion* – a 240,000 ton oil tanker. I had thought that the ships at Thompson's were big at 150,000 tons but the size of this oil tanker was phenomenal. I can remember the plate was so heavy that hydraulic jacks had to be used to fair-up almost everything. As construction progressed, huge heavy duty nets were strewn across the centre tanks to prevent certain death for any unfortunate worker who fell from deck head staging. I must admit that the safety nets gave me much more confidence when working at those great heights. When I worked on the Wear safety nets weren't used.

'There were the characters, of course – every shipyard had them. But one who stands out in my memory is 'Clogger', so called because he wore wooden clogs for work, the likes of which I hadn't seen before – or since.

'I enjoyed my experience at the Wallsend yard and I can honestly say that I was treated fairly there. I often wondered what happened to Ted.'

In 1976 Doxford's at Pallion in Sunderland built the world's largest covered shipyard. This new yard replaced old gantries and berths that had been built in 1904 and meant that workers were protected from the worst of the weather conditions. At the time, the covered yard was said to be one of the most up-to-date in the world.

The *Nessbank* under construction at the indoor yard of Doxford's in the 1970s.

The *Riverbank* being towed out of Doxford's into the River Wear in 1977.

Right: An advert for 'the cargo ship of the 70s' – the SD14 (shelterdecker of 14,000 tons dwt). The SD14 was designed by Sunderland company Austin & Pickersgill's with the first ship being launched in 1967. The design became a successful Wearside export and was used by shipbuilders throughout the world. In 1982 the 200th SD14 was launched in Brazil. The last SD14 built on the Wear was the *Sunderland Venture* in 1983.

Far right: The first day of construction of a SD14.

The launch of a completed SD14 at Sunderland.

Right: The Austin & Pickersgill's shipyard on the cover of one of their company magazines in 1978.

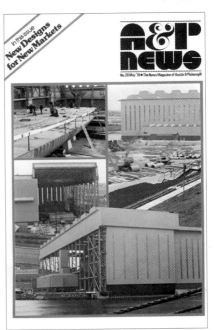

Sporting Memories

Right: An advert for 'The Fight of a Lifetime' – Muhammad Ali versus Joe Frazier at Madison Square Garden in 1971. It is interesting that Ali is advertised under his former name Cassius Clay. 'Muhammad Ali' is included underneath but in small letters. Such was the interest in the bout throughout the world that it was broadcast in cinemas such as the Odeon in Newcastle at 2 am. The price of seats ranged from £2 10 shillings to £6 six shillings. Ali lost this bout but three years later he beat George Foreman in the 'Rumble in the Jungle' to once again become the Heavyweight Champion of the World.

In 1977 Muhammad Ali visited the North East and drew massive crowds wherever he went. When he came to Newcastle twelve-year-old Audrey Guthrie (a future boxer herself) went to see him:

'It was an exciting time and I wanted to be part of it. He was making a visit to the old Grainger Park Boys' Club in Newcastle and I was determined to see him. There was a big crowd outside the club and everyone was amazed that he was here in Newcastle. I was only small and when I saw him I couldn't believe how big he was – he was like a giant. And he looked so strong. He was wearing a jacket but I could see how solid he was with huge shoulders. I knew he was a boxer but that didn't mean much to me at that time. I never dreamt that twenty years later I would become a boxer and the first professional woman in the North East.'

Left: Former Middlesbrough player Frank Spraggon challenges Pele in a match in the North American Soccer League in the 1970s. At this time some of the biggest names in football were being signed by American clubs. Alongside Pele there were players such as Eusebio, Franz Beckenbauer, George Best, Rodney Marsh, Johan Cruyff and Bobby Moore – although most were past their best. A number of footballers from the North East also played in America. Two of these were former Newcastle player Paul Cannell and Dennis Tueart who played for Sunderland and Manchester City.

Below: Paul Cannell and Dennis Tueart on stickers produced by Pannini in the 1970s.

Basketball has been played in the Britain since the late 19th century but the sport took off in the North East when a team was formed in Sunderland in 1976. The team played under a number of names depending on sponsorship – Epab Sunderland, Sunblest Sunderland, Sunderland Saints and Sunderland Maestros are just a few of the titles. The side played home games at the Sporting Club of Washington (*left*) before moving to Crowtree Leisure Centre in Sunderland. Their golden era was in the early 1980s when Sunderland twice won the National Basketball League Play Offs in 1981 and '83 at Wembley Arena.

Left: This advert from 1977 is offering 'All-star American style razzamatas' at Sunderland's National League Division Two match. The admission was 40 pence (20 pence for children).

Right: Two North East sporting legends – Brendan Foster and Jackie Milburn. Foster competed in three Olympic Games with his best finish being the bronze medal he won in the 10,000 metres at Montreal in 1976. Two years previously he set the world record for the 3,000 metres at the 'Gateshead Games'. This was the first major athletics event at the Gateshead International Stadium. In 1977 Foster helped to organise the Gateshead Fun Run that was one of the first events of its kind in Britain. Four years later he founded the Great North Run.

The Not So Fun Run

In the late 1970s I took part in the Metro Radio Fun Run – it was one of a number of races at that time to encourage people to 'run for fun'. It was a last minute decision for me to take part and I lined-up with the other junior runners in the clothes I came in – jeans and a T-shirt. It was a hot day and I was struggling in my clothes so half way round I took off my T-shirt to finish the race bare-chested. The photograph on the right shows me proudly showing the certificate for completing the run. I'm not sure what happened to my T-shirt!

Andrew Clark

25

TV Times

Right: A 1973 advert for a television from Telefusion Rentals which had shops in Newcastle, South Shields and Wallsend. In those days many people rented their TVs rather than buy them outright. They are advertising a colour, 22 inch set for £1.61 a week. In the 1970s there were only three television channels – BBC 1, BBC 2 and ITV – and it was common for some programmes to be watched by over 20 million people. Popular shows in the decade included:

Comedies: Citizen Smith, Dad's Army, Fawlty Towers, George and Mildred, The Good Life, Man About The House, On The Buses, Rising Damp, Steptoe and Son, To The Manor Born.

Dramas: Colditz, Crown Court, Grange Hill, Rock Follies, The Sweeney, Upstairs Downstairs.

American shows: Charlie's Angels, Columbo, Happy Days, Kojak, Kung Fu, Little House on the Prairie, MASH, Rockford Files, The Waltons.

Quizes and other shows: Family Fortunes, Generation Game, Mastermind, Nationwide, New Faces, That's Life, The Krypton Factor.

Left: The Likely Lads – Terry Collier and Bob Ferris – played by James Bolam and Rodney Bewes. *Whatever Happened to the Likely Lads* ran for two series in 1973 and '74. Perhaps the favourite episode was 'No Hiding Place' where the two lads spend all day trying to avoid the result of an England game so they can watch it on television that evening. The series was written by Dick Clement and Ian La Frenais who also in the 1970s wrote *Porridge* staring Ronnie Barker and Richard Beckinsale.

In 1970 Kate Adie left her job at BBC Radio Durham to take up a position at Radio Bristol. After disc jockey Kenny Everett was sacked from Radio One he joined the West Country station and Kate was his producer but as she was later to admit she was more his tea lady. Kate worked alongside a number of people who were helping out at the radio station who went on to become famous. Before becoming a household name for his appearances in *Blackadder* and on *Time Team*, Tony Robinson was earning the occasional £2 a week at Radio Bristol. Diana Moran was another who helped out at the station before finding fame on Breakfast Television as the Green Goddess.

In the mid '70s Kate Adie moved into TV herself, first with BBC South West at Plymouth then BBC South at Southampton before joining the National News and becoming one of the most familiar faces on the small screen.

Kate had been adopted as a baby by Sunderland pharmacist John Adie and his wife Maud. After studying at Sunderland Church High School and Newcastle University Kate began her media career at BBC Radio Durham in 1969.

The North East drama *When the Boat Comes In* was a very popular series in the 1970s. With its memorable theme tune – *Dance ti thy Daddy* sung by Gateshead-born Alex Glasgow – the show followed the lives of Jack Ford and the Seaton family in the fictional Tyneside town of Gallowshields. Most of the stories centred around the character of Jack Ford, a soldier returning to civilian life after the First World War and his experiences of the hard times of the 1920s. He was played by Sunderland-born James Bolam who has had a television career that has spanned six decades with appearances in *Only When I Laugh*, *The Beiderbeck Affair*, *Born and Bred*, *New Tricks* and *Grandpa in My Pocket*.

Other North East actors in *When the Boat Comes In* included Edward Wilson (South Shields), James Garbutt (Houghton-le-Spring) and Jean Heywood (Blyth). In the first episode of the show there was an early appearance by Richard Griffiths. The Thornaby-born actor was a regular on TV in the 1980s and '90s and was in the award-winning play *The History Boys*. Griffiths was also known around the world as Vernon Dursley in the Harry Potter films.

The main cast from the first series of *When the Boat Come In*. Left to right: Billy Seaton (Edward Wilson), Jack Ford (James Bolam), Jessie Seaton (Susan Jameson), Tom Seaton (John Nightingale), Mary Seaton (Michelle Newell), Bill Seaton (James Garbutt) and Bella Seaton (Jean Heywood).

When the Boat Comes In was created by South Shields writer James Mitchell who wrote the majority of the scripts for the four series that ran from 1976 to 1981. Other writers on the show were North Shields playwright Tom Hadaway, Shildon author Sid Chaplin as well as Alex Glasgow. James Mitchell had a very successful television career. He created the spy series *Callan* staring Edward Woodward and also wrote for *Z Cars* and *The Avengers* in the 1960s.

Right: *The Paper Lads* was a children's series produced by Tyne Tees Television from 1977 to '79. The memorable theme tune *Back Home Once Again* was performed by Renaissance whose biggest hit was *Northern Lights* in 1978.

The September 1977 issue of the magazine *Look-in* gave this description of the series:

'Have you been keeping your file open on *The Paper Lads* ... J.G., Baz, Gog, Ian and Sam ... the sharp-eyed, quick-witted bunch of Tyneside youngsters, from Tyne Tees Television's exciting new drama series.

'As you probably know by now, these youngsters are a match for anyone as they prove in their lively adventures screened against the dramatic Tyneside skyline.

'For those who haven't seen the series, *The Paper Lads* are a group of Tyneside youngsters who earn their pocket money by delivering newspapers. Their exploits and intimate human stories touch on the hopes, disappointments and achievements of children growing up amid the bustle and vigour of modern city life. What makes these youngsters different is the man who employs them, ex-policeman Jack Crawford (played by Glynn Edwards).

'He has taught them to use their eyes and ears, their common sense, their intelligence and, when necessary, their hearts. For a paper lad with his wits about him is as tuned to his district as the old-fashioned copper on the beat.'

Sounds of the 1970s

An advert from 1972 for 'Progressive Friday' at the Mayfair in Newcastle. The Velvet Underground and Geordie were appearing and admission was 60 pence before 10 pm and 70 pence afterwards.

Geordie were a four-piece rock group formed in Newcastle in 1972 and they enjoyed success throughout the '70s. The group's singer Brian Johnson joined AC/DC in 1980 and achieved worldwide fame with one of the biggest bands in the world.

Left: The cover of Lindisfarne's single *Meet Me on the Corner* that reached number five in the charts in 1972 and won the prestigious Ivor Novello award. The Tyneside band were formed in the late 1960s and their debut album was *Nicely Out of Tune*, released in 1970. The line up at that time was Alan Hull, Ray Jackson, Simon Cowe, Rod Clements and Ray Laidlaw.

Meet Me On the Corner had come from their chart-topping second album *Fog on The Tyne*. The title track from this album became another classic from the band. They also had top ten hit singles with *Lady Eleanor* and *Run for Home*.

Lindisfarne became known for their Christmas concerts at the City Hall in Newcastle.

Alan Price originally found fame with the Animals in the 1960s but he also had a successful solo career. His biggest hit of the 1970s

was *Jarrow Song* based on the march from South Tyneside to London in 1936. The Jarrow Crusade (*seen right*) was a protest against the high unemployment and poverty the town was suffering at the time.

In 1973 Price wrote the soundtrack and had a small role in the film *O Lucky Man* starring Malcolm McDowell. Two years later Price played the title character in *Alfie Darling* which was a sequel to *Alfie,* one of Michael Caine's most successful films of the 1960s.

Right: An advert from 1972 for the RCA factory in Washington. The American company had the 'first fully automatic record press in Britain' for its vinyl seven and twelve inch discs. The advert also boasts 'a lot of big names through our presses'. Some of those on the list are not so popular today as they were in the 1970s. Artists such as Leontyne Price, Artur Rubinstein and Eugene Ormandy are hardly household names now. Sixth on the list is Elvis Presley who five years later would save the factory from closure. When 'The King' tragically died in August 1977 there was a surge in sales of his recordings and the RCA plant in Washington worked overtime to meet the demand. The boom for Elvis Presley records did not last and in 1981 RCA closed its factory in Washington. At its peak the plant employed 300 workers.

Right: Ten years after Elvis' death this copy of the *Radio Times* proclaimed: 'Long live THE KING'.

We're putting a lot of big names through our presses.

RCA who record such names as Eugene Ormandy, André Previn Leontyne Price, Artur Rubinstein The Archies, Elvis Presley Jim Reeves, Clodagh Rodgers Nina Simone and many others have built the first fully automatic record press in Britain. And it's right here in Washington, County Durham. It can produce records faster than any other press. And RCA provide the fastest record delivery service in Britain. We're pretty proud of that . . . and so is Washington.

RCA Limited, Record Division,
Manufacturing Plant,
Armstrong Industrial Estate,
WASHINGTON, Co. Durham, England.
Telephone: 0632-461511 & 0632-461521

RCA

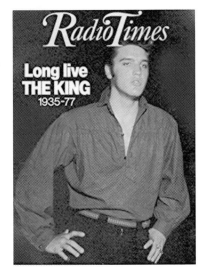

The Police became one of the biggest bands of the late 1970s and early '80s with hits such as Roxanne (*left*). The band members were Stewart Copeland (drums), Andy Summers (guitar) and Sting (Wallsend-born Gordon Sumner) on vocals and bass. Sting went on to further success with his solo career and also appeared in a number of Hollywood movies. In 2013 he recorded the album *The Last Ship* inspired by his memories of growing up on Tyneside.

The music world was changed forever when punk exploded on to the scene in the mid 1970s. One of the earliest punk bands in the North East were the Angelic Upstarts from South Shields. Their first album *Teenage Warning* (*left*) reached number 29 in the charts in 1979.

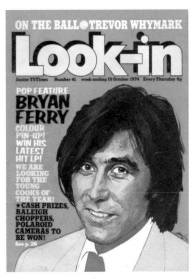

Washington-born Bryan Ferry made the cover of the popular 1970s music magazine *Look-in*. Ferry left the region in the late 1960s and formed Roxy Music in 1971. Hits singles in the '70s included *Virginia Plain*, *Love is the Drug* and *Dance Away*.

The *Look-in* magazine was launched in 1971 as a children's version of the *TV Times*. As well as articles about television it also featured music, films and sport.

Childhood Toys and Games

Christmas Memories

In the photograph on the right I am with my younger sister and brother at Binns in South Shields at Christmas in 1979. We've just been given our toys from Santa Claus and it looks like I have a toy doctor's kit. I can't remember what my sister received and my little baby brother isn't very happy to sit on Santa's knee.

My Mam made Christmas very special for us. We would wake up very excited on Christmas morning at 5 am and rush downstairs into the living room to see what Santa had brought. On each chair our toys were all wrapped nicely and placed for the three of us. We used to get one big toy each and lots of smaller ones such as games and teddies. Also every year we would have our three stockings that Mam hung from the mantle of the fireplace. Inside we would find an apple, orange, nuts, small toys and some sweets. My favourite toy was the Strawberry Shortcake doll (*right*) and I loved her hat and hair as it had the lovely smell of strawberries.

Sharyn Taylor

Left: Strawberry Shortcake dolls were launched in 1979 and were one of the best selling toys that Christmas. They continued to be popular in the '80s.

The toys available from Binns in 1972 were a Silver Cross dolls pram for £22.13, Subbuteo table soccer game for £3.50 and Plasticraft (for making jewellery) for £2.75.

Left: A Space Hopper – one of the iconic toys from the 1970s. It was invented in 1968 by an Italian company who manufactured rubber balls. Called a Space Hopper in Britain, in other parts of the world they have names such as 'Pon-pon', 'Hoppity Hop', 'Hippity Hop' or simply 'Sit n Bounce'.

Right: Another memorable toy from the '70s were clackers – two hard plastic balls attached with string. They were held in the hand and the idea was to make the balls swing to get them to hit each other above and below your hand. It would hurt if the balls hit you and they were eventually withdrawn from sale.

AIRFIX-72 SCALE
SUNDERLAND III

BIONIC™ POWER ARM

BIONIC™ EYE   BIONIC™ ARM MODULES

Above: The Airfix model for the Sunderland Flying Boat that was assembled from small pieces of plastic, glued together and painted. In the mid 1970s over 20 million model kits were being sold a year.

Right: The football game Subbuteo, where you flick your small players, was launched in 1949. It was the top selling football game for decades until the competition from video games saw Subbuteo taken off the market for several years. It was relaunched in 2012.

The Six Million Dollar Man action figure with bionic eye and power arm. Other figures at that time included Action Man, Doctor Who and Spock & Kirk from Star Trek.

Toys of the 1970s

Any child of the 1970s will remember their favourite toys. Here are some from the decade; many are still around today:

Hungry Hippos (one of the best sellers of 1978), Frustration, Battling Robots, Simon, Spirograph, Etch-a-Sketch, Weebles, Stretch Armstrong, Mastermind, Evel Knievel, Big Trak, Othello, Slinkys, Speak & Spell, Operation and KerPlunk.

Comics

My favourite comic in the 1970s was the Tiger (*right*) that had sports stories such as Roy of the Rovers, Billy's Boots and Hot Shot Hamish. Other comics at the time included: Action, Warlord, Victor, Krazy, Beezer, Whizzor and Chips, Whoopee!, Mandy and Debbie. In 1977 a new science fiction comic called 2000AD (*far right*) was being launched and the week the first edition was published I hurried to buy a copy. When I arrived at the newsagent I was told that they had just sold the last comic. 2000AD became one of the most popular comics in Britain and one of its characters, Judge Dredd, was made into a film with Sylvester Stallone. I sometimes look on Ebay and see copies of that first edition on offer for thousands of pounds.

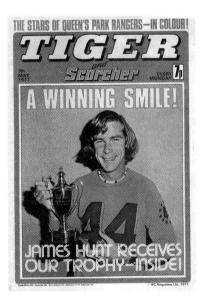

THE STARS OF QUEEN'S PARK RANGERS—IN COLOUR!
TIGER and Scorcher
A WINNING SMILE!
JAMES HUNT RECEIVES OUR TROPHY—INSIDE!

No.1 2000AD FEATURING THE NEW Dan Dare
FREE SPACE SPINNER
SPACE-AGE DINOSAURS!

Andrew Clark

Left: One of the highlights of the gifts on offer at Binns for Christmas 1972 was the Raleigh Chopper. The bike cost £34.50 or Binns were offering a nine month credit sale at no extra cost. The Chopper was described as: 'The racy little Sports Cycle from Raleigh that every boy would love.'

Raleigh launched the Chopper in 1970 and it was an immediate hit with its distinctive shape, wide tyres, long seat, high handlebars, cross bar gear stick and different size wheels – 16 inches at the front and 20 inches at the back. The Chopper was sold throughout the 1970s but ceased production in 1982. It was brought back in 2004 but the gear changer was moved from the cross bar to handlebars making it safer.

Life on Two Wheels

If one bike sums up the 1970s it has to be the Raleigh Chopper but there were a number of other popular bikes as well. For my first bike, I was too small for a Chopper so my parents bought me the next best thing – a Tomahawk (it cost about £30). This was a smaller version of the Chopper and I remember mine was purple. The other bike in this series was the Budgie and my younger sister had an orange one.

My next bike was a Raleigh Commando which was like an early BMX. I thought it was a good bike – it was black and had a great name like the comics I used to read at the time. The gears were changed using a twist grip on the handle bar and so much safer than the Chopper's gear stick.

My sister for her next bike, after her Budgie, got a Raleigh Grifter (*above*) which was even more like the BMXs which were soon to become very common. I seem to remember the Grifter was quite a heavy bike compared to my Commando. The junior versions of the Grifter were the Strika and the Boxer.

My next bike was a Racer but I missed my Commando. Like a lot of the bikes at the time it had a long seat which was great for giving 'backas'.

Andrew Clark

Left: The Commando from one of a series of adverts from Raleigh that compared their designs to classic British inventions and engineering. In this photograph the Commando bike is alongside a Royal Flying Corps biplane. A similar advert for the Raleigh Chopper had a hovercraft in the background. Raleigh gave this description of the Commando: 'For 7 to 11 year olds, a bike as tough, tenacious and stylish as they come. And it's equally popular with the little girls in your family too. But though it might seem all good looks, depend on it that the Raleigh Commando is ultra-reliable too.'

Above: A wonderful photograph of a 'bogie' race in Scotswood, Newcastle in 1975. These go-carts were home-made from old pram wheels and spare bits of wood. In those days few homes had the drills and other power tools we take for granted today. Holes in the wood were probably burnt out with a red hot poker from the fire.

Right: Rounders in the yard of Chester Road School, Sunderland in the late '70s. A hula hoop is being used as the 'base'. Another popular game was back lane cricket with an old rubbish bin for a wicket. (A modern wheelie bin would have been no good.) It was one handed catches off the wall and 'six and out' if you hit the ball into someone's backyard.

Right: This looks like a game of 'pirates' at Canning Street School, Newcastle in 1971. The game was played by getting out all the gym equipment which you stood on, sat on and hung from (as can be seen in the photograph). Two people would then go around and try to catch and 'tig' you. You were out of the game if you were tigged or you touched the floor.

Days to Remember

Lambton Lion Park, near Chester-le-Street, was open between 1972 and 1980. Visitors would drive through the park to see the animals close up and for many the highlight was the baboons who sometimes would climb on your car (*above*). Other animals included lions,

elephants, camels, giraffes, zebras and white rhino. The park was a joint venture between the Lambton Estate and the Chipperfield Circus family.

Another attraction at Lambton Lion Park was an old Viscount plane that you could go inside. It was later moved to Saltwell Park in Gateshead (*left*) and was there until 1993.

Left: An advert for a Polaroid Square Shooter Camera from Woolco in Killingworth Township. The Polaroid was a camera that produced instant photographs and the price for this one in 1971 was £15.95 with the film costing £1.59.

Two young ladies have their photograph taken while holding monkeys in King Street, South Shields around 1975. Photographers would use animals, props or people in costumes and offer you the chance to have your picture taken with them for a small fee.

Our First Holiday

The photograph on the right shows Dad, me, sister Paula and Mam on our first family holiday in September 1973. We spent a week at Butlins in Filey and stayed in a hut similar to the one that is behind us. I don't remember too much about the holiday but I'm guessing it wasn't that warm in North Yorkshire that year as we are wearing coats and jumpers. The postcard below was posted in 1976 and shows the indoor and outdoor pool at Filey. Other attractions at Butlins at that time were the amusements and rides. There's a great action photograph of me sliding down the helter-skelter on a mat on page 6.

Andrew Clark

Billy Butlin started building his holiday camp in Filey in 1939 but because of the Second World War it was not opened to the public until 1945. The camp could accommodate over 10,000 visitors at a time and in 1975 there were 175,000 people who stayed there. The Filey camp closed in 1983 but there are still Butlins camps at Minehead, Skegness and Bognor Regis.

Right: An advert from 1973 offering 'Sun and Fun' with South Shields travel agent Graham and Warren. By the early 1970s foreign holidays were becoming more common and The 'New Destinations for '73' included:

Spain, Costa Del Sol, 15 days from £61
Greece, Corfu, 15 days from £66
Tunisia, Sousse, 14 nights from £68
Ibiza, 14 nights from £53
Yugoslavia, 2 weeks from £55
Jersey, 1 week from £32

Graham and Warren travel agents were offering direct flights from Newcastle Airport (*below*).

Workers run out of Laing's shipyard in Sunderland in 1979. There are plenty of smiles on their faces as this was the start of the shipyard fortnight holiday. Within a decade of this happy scene every yard on the Wear would be closed. Laing's launched its last ship in 1985 then three years later centuries of shipbuilding in the town came to an end with the closure of the last yards.

A very busy scene in Durham for the Miners' Gala in the 1970s. A brass band and lodge banner makes its way through the crowd while three fashionable teenagers dance arm-in-arm. As the pits of County Durham closed less miners, their families and banners attended the 'Big Meeting'. However, in recent years many former mining communities have had their banners restored with the help of Heritage Lottery Funding. Now more banners are paraded through Durham than have been seen for decades and crowds flock to the Gala.

American President Jimmy Carter shaking hands outside Newcastle Civic Centre on 6th May 1977. The President was on a whistle stop tour of the North East and his other destinations were Cornings Glass in Sunderland and Washington Old Hall. At the ancestral home of the first American President, Carter was presented with a miner's lamp. In Newcastle he received the Freedom of the City with the words: 'Mr President, sir, you are a Georgian. You have now become a Geordie.' Famously, the former peanut farmer from Georgia delighted the crowds at the Civic Centre by shouting 'Howay the Lads'. The President left the region on his plane, Air Force One, from Newcastle Airport.

Five lads from Arthur's Hill in Newcastle raising money with 'Penny for the Guy'. The guy was made with some old clothes that were stuffed and tied together and this one looks like it has a football as a head. The few coppers donated by passers by was normally spent on buying some fireworks. In the weeks before Guy Fawkes Night on the 5th November, bits of wood or old furniture were collected for the bonfire that was often put together on some waste ground. On Bonfire Night it was lit and a few fireworks set off with people holding sparklers.

In the 1970s Bonfire Night was a real highlight for young 'uns in the dark nights waiting for Christmas to come. Halloween, meanwhile, was a much smaller affair than it is now. There were no trick or treating, no parties or fancy dress costumes like there is today. Halloween in this country has become much more like America with even pumpkins being sold in their thousands. Kids in the 1970s had to make do with an old hollowed-out turnip with a candle in it. Pupils from Redby School in Sunderland show off their turnip Halloween lanterns on the right.

Above: A great photograph of Andrew Backhouse with a couple of sparklers on Bonfire Night at Middlesbrough in 1979.

Left: In 1974 pupils from Ryhope Comprehensive made the front cover of the *New Music Express* when they produced their version of the rock opera *Tommy* by The Who.

Wembley Dreams

Left: Sunderland manager Bob Stokoe after his side's victory at Wembley in the FA Cup Final in 1973. Second Division Sunderland had defied the odds by beating Leeds United 1-0 to lift the Cup. The Yorkshire side were one of the strongest teams in the country at that time and a Second Division club had not won the FA Cup for over 40 years. At the final whistle, Stokoe famously ran on to the pitch to embrace goalkeeper Jimmy Montgomery. Bob Stokoe had also won the Cup as a player with Newcastle United in 1955. His assistant, Billy Elliott, is holding the base of the cup as they go on a lap of honour.

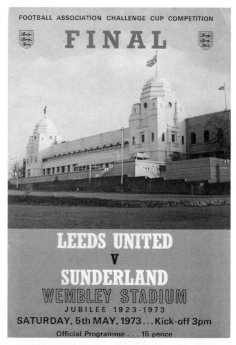

Above: Sunderland captain Bobby Kerr holds up the FA Cup after victory over Leeds. Goalkeeper Jimmy Montgomery can just be seen with the Cup's lid on his head. He made a magnificent double save in the second half to keep the score at 1-0. The goalscorer that day was Ian Porterfield.

Right: Workers at the Rediffusion factory in Murton, County Durham, show their support for Sunderland in 1973. There's lots of red and white on display and even a home-made cup being held by a couple of supporters.

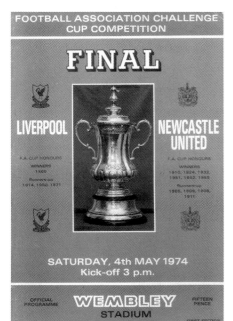

A year after Sunderland's FA Cup win it was Newcastle's turn to represent the region at Wembley. Unfortunately, the Cup was not to return to the North East as the Magpies were beaten 3-0 by Liverpool with Kevin Keegan scoring twice.

The Newcastle squad from the early 1970s. Joe Harvey (standing far left) was the manager at the time. He had led Newcastle to FA Cup glory as captain in 1951 and '52. As a manager his finest hour was taking Newcastle to European victory in the Fairs Cup in 1969. Included in the photograph above are Malcolm Macdonald, Bobby Moncur, Frank Clark, Terry Hibbert, Terry McDermott, 'Jinky' Jimmy Smith and Willie McFaul – who all played in the FA Cup Final at Wembley in 1974.

Malcolm Macdonald on the cover of the League Football magazine in 1972. 'Supermac' was signed from Luton in 1971 and made an immediate impact on his debut – scoring a hat-trick. The centre forward stayed at St James' Park for five years before he was sold to Arsenal for £333,333.

Above: After defeat at Wembley in 1974, the fans gave a heroes welcome to the players when they returned to Newcastle. Two years later, this time in the League Cup, Newcastle were again beaten in a Wembley Final. The victorious side were Manchester City with the winning goal scored by Newcastle-born Dennis Tueart with an overhead kick.

Right: Before the days of the internet or television sports channels, most football fans relied on buying the 'Football Pink' on a Saturday to get the latest scores.

There was a third team from the North East who had dreams of Wembley in the 1970s and that was Blyth Spartans. The club from the Northern League went on a fairy tale FA Cup run that saw them reach the fifth round, beating much bigger clubs on the way and just missed out on a match with the mighty Arsenal.

Blyth had to win four qualifying matches before the first round of the FA Cup and they did so against local sides Shildon, Crook, Consett and Bishop Auckland. Then there were victories in the first three rounds proper against Burscough, Chesterfield and Enfield before Blyth were drawn away to Stoke City. The Spartans won 3-2. Cup fever now gripped the North East and the Spartans made headlines throughout the country. The next game was away to Wrexham and 8,000 supporters made the long journey to the Racecourse Ground. Blyth were winning for most of the game until a disputed goal gave the Welsh side a draw and a replay. The Wrexham goal came after a corner was retaken when the corner flag fell down.

Left: Terry Johnson scores for Blyth Spartans against Wrexham at the Racecourse Ground in the fifth round tie of the FA Cup in 1978.

For the replay against Wrexham the tie was moved to Newcastle United's St James' Park and 43,000 people filled the stadium. The town of Blyth at that time had a total population of 36,000 so the Spartans were roared on by supporters from throughout the North East. Wrexham took a 2-0 lead then Terry Johnson pulled a goal back but even with the backing of a passionate crowd the equaliser never came. Blyth were out of the FA Cup and the dream was over. If they had won, their next opponents would have been Arsenal at Roker Park.

The programme for Blyth's FA Cup replay against Wrexham at St James' Park in 1978. On the cover are Dave Clarke, Ron Guthrie and Terry Johnson. Former Newcastle player Ron Guthrie was a FA Cup winner with Sunderland in 1973.

In the days before videos and dvds football fans would buy radio recordings of commentaries of important games. Here is BBC Radio Newcastle's 'A souvenir in sound of Blyth Spartans Historic FA Cup run 1977-78'. This record has been signed by the Spartans players.

Snapshots of the 1970s

Right: To mark the 150th anniversary of the Stockton and Darlington Railway there was a cavalcade of locomotives at Shildon on 31st August 1975.

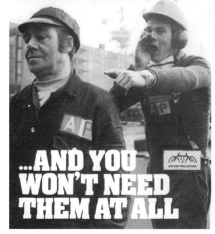

An advert produced by Austin & Pickersgill's shipyard on the Wear warning of the dangers of noise in the workplace. In the 1960s and '70s there was a change in attitude towards industrial health and safety with measures introduced to protect workers.

The famous 'Flying Scotsman' made an appearance at Shildon in 1975 and crowds lined the track to see it and the other locomotives

Goalmouth action from the derby match between Sunderland and Newcastle at Roker Park, 8th April 1977 – the game finished 2-2. Sunderland were relegated from the First Division, as it was then called, at the end of that season. Earlier in the decade both clubs had reached FA Cup Finals at Wembley but Newcastle and Sunderland ended the 1970s in the Second Division.

Youngsters take part in an egg and spoon race during a party in Westbury Street, Sunderland in 1977. The party was to celebrate the Silver Jubilee of Queen Elizabeth who had been on the throne for twenty-five years. Street parties like this were held around the country and many took place on the special Jubilee public holiday on 7th June. On that day over a million people lined the streets of London as the Queen and Prince Philip, in the golden state coach, led a procession from Buckingham

Palace to St Paul's Cathedral. The Queen also went on to tour the Commonwealth visiting Australia, New Zealand, Canada, India and a number of Caribbean and Pacific Islands. Between May and August there were royal engagements throughout Britain and on the 14th and 15th July the Queen and Prince Philip came to the North East.

In 1977 Pauline Clark was living in Cramlington and could not miss the opportunity of seeing the Queen and Prince Philip on their visit to the town on 15th July:

Waving the Union Jack in their back garden in Cramlington on the 15th July 1977 are Andrew and Paula Clark.

'The Queen arrived by train at Cramlington Railway Station and a large black car took her and Prince Philip off to the town centre to officially open Concordia Leisure Centre. The route from the station was lined with crowds of people waiting for a glimpse of the Queen. I sat by the road near our home for ages with my two children, Andrew and Paula. As the car drove past we all waved and I am sure Prince Philip was waving back at me in reply. Once their duties in Cramlington were over the Royal party stayed the night at Alnwick Castle as guests of the Duke of Northumberland. That day there were dozens of street parties in Cramlington and we had one where we lived.

'Forty years later I love watching TV programmes or reading books about the Royal family. One time when I was on holiday in Norfolk I went on a tour of Sandringham House, one of the Queen's residences.'

During 1977 a number of places were named 'Jubilee' to commemorate the occasion such as the Jubilee Line – the London underground line that was under construction at the time. In Newcastle the pub the Man in the Moon was renamed the Jubilee. In the photograph on the right there is an image of a crown and '77'. The pub in Princess Square is now called Trillians Rock Bar.

Remember You're A Womble

The photograph on the right shows me with my Mam and a huge toy Womble. It looks as big as me! Wombles were everywhere in the 1970s. The Wombles started off in books by Elisabeth Beresford then they had a TV show and even a film was made in 1977 called *Wombling Free*.

The original television show ran for two series and was narrated by Bernard Cribbins. The Womble characters included: Great Uncle Bulgaria, Bungo, Tobermory, Orinoco, Tomsk, Wellington and Madame Cholet. They lived on Wimbledon Common and spent their time picking up rubbish and recycling.

The theme music was written by Mike Batt who later formed the band The Wombles dressing up as the characters. They had top ten hits with *The Wombling Song* and *Remember You're A Womble*. Batt also wrote the song *Bright Eyes* for the film version of *Watership Down*. He later worked with artists such as Steeleye Span, Alvin Stardust, Vanessa Mae and Katie Melua.

Sharyn Taylor

Dressed as Wombles, this Women's Institute float promoted the Keep Britain Tidy Campaign in Sunderland in the 1970s.

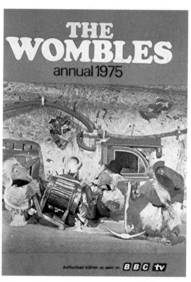

The Wombles annual from 1975. They made a television comeback in the 1990s with an animated series.

Another popular children's television series from the 1960s and '70s was *Chigley*. This was one of three stop-motion productions that also included *Trumpton* and *Camberwick Green*. They all featured small communities with characters such as Windy Miller and the firemen Pugh, Pugh, Barney McGrew, Cuthbert, Dibble and Grub. For Christmas 1972 moving puppets from Chigley were used for the window display at Fenwick's in Newcastle.

In 1978 Bobby Thompson released his album *The Little Waster*. Recorded at Ryhope Poplars Club and the Mayfair Ballroom it captured the comedian's unique brand of North East humour.

Right: An advert for the Makro Store in Washington from 1979. The giant store was publicising its new 20,000 square foot extension that offered 10,000 different food lines and 15,000 non food lines to its trade customers. The store for 'North East traders and businessmen' was opened in Washington in September 1973 and is still trading today.

In the late 1970s Vaux Breweries were promoting a number of their products in this advert. Included are Double Maxim and Samson which since the closure of Vaux in 1999 are now produced at the Maxim Brewery in Houghton-le-Spring.

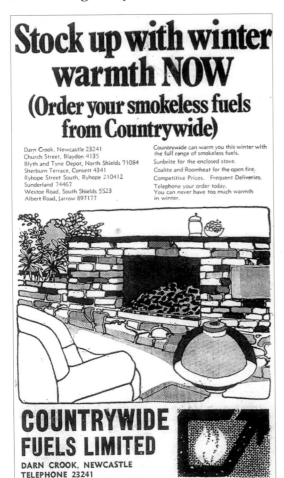

A wintery scene at Greenside, near Ryton, in 1978. One of the coldest winters on record was in 1978/79 – also known as the 'Winter of Discontent' for the number of strikes at that time. For cold winter nights in the 1970s there was nothing better than being in front of a warm coal fire (*left*).

1970s Time Line

1970

April 10th – Paul McCartney announces that he has left the Beatles.

April 13th – An oxygen tank on the Apollo 13 spacecraft explodes. Four days later the crew return safely to Earth.

June 14th – England's are knocked out of the World Cup in Mexico with a 3-2 defeat to West Germany. Brazil win the tournament, beating Italy in the final.

June 18th – The Conservative Party wins the General Election and Edward Heath becomes Prime Minister. Labour had been in power for six years.

September 19th – The first Glastonbury Festival (called at that time Worthy Farm Festival) is held. Tyrannosaurus Rex were the headliners.

October 19th – BP announce the discovery of a large oil field under the North Sea.

November 22nd – The ten shilling note ceased to be legal tender (*below*).

Prime Minister Harold Wilson officially opens the St Cuthbert's Village housing development in Gateshead on 17th April 1970.

1971

January 2nd – Sixty-six football supporters are killed after a stairway crush at Ibrox Stadium in Glasgow during the Rangers versus Celtic match.

February 15th – Decimal Day when pounds and 'new' pence replace pounds, shillings and pence.

March 10th – The film *Get Carter* is released.

September 1st – The pre-decimal penny and threepence ceased to be legal tender.

September 21st – The television music show *The Old Grey Whistle Test* is broadcast for the first time on BBC 2.

October 1st – Disney World in Florida is opened.

1972

January 30th – British soldiers kill 13 people in Londonderry, Northern Ireland, on Bloody Sunday.

February 25th – A seven-week miners' strike comes to an end.

June 5th – The funeral of the Duke of Windsor (formerly Edward VIII).

September 1st – The school leaving age in England and Wales is raised to 16 years. Prefabricated huts are used to help accommodate pupils.

November 29th – Atari releases *Pong*, the first video game to achieve commercial success.

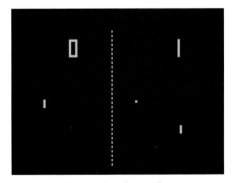

Pong was a simple video game of bats and a ball allowing an electronic version of tennis, hockey/football or squash.

1973

January 1st – Britain joins the European Economic Community, which later becomes the European Union.

March 1st – Pink Floyd release their album *The Dark Side of the Moon*.

March 29th – The last United States soldier leaves Vietnam.

May 5th – Sunderland beat Leeds United 1-0 in the FA Cup final at Wembley. Ian Porterfield scores the only goal of the game.

October 17th – England draw 1-1 against Poland at Wembley and fail to qualify for the 1974 World Cup.

1974

February 28th – The General Election results in a hung Parliament with Labour having the most seats. Edward Heath resigns and Harold Wilson becomes Prime Minister.

April 1st – The Local Government Act 1972 comes into effect in England and Wales. There are major changes to the councils throughout the North East. North Tyneside and South Tyneside Councils are created and join with Newcastle, Gateshead and Sunderland to form Tyne & Wear Metropolitan County Council.

May 4th – Liverpool beat Newcastle United 3-0 to win the FA Cup Final. Kevin Keegan scores two of the goals.

August 8th – US President Richard Nixon announces his resignation following the Watergate scandal. Gerald Ford becomes President.

September 23rd – Ceefax is started by the BBC – the world's first teletext information service.

October 10th – The second General Election of the year. Labour wins a small majority of three seats.

October 30th – In 'The Rumble in the Jungle' Muhammad Ali defeats George Foreman in Zaire to become Heavyweight Champion of the World.

November 7th – Lord Lucan disappears after the murder of his children's nanny.

December – Brendan Foster is voted BBC Sports Personality of the Year. Earlier in the year he won the gold medal in the 5,000 metres at the European Champions.

Muhammad Ali.

1975

February 11th – Margaret Thatcher becomes leader of the Conservative Party.

February 13th – The miners accept a 35% pay rise offer from the Government.

April 4th – Microsoft is founded by Bill Gates and Paul Allen

April 30th – The Vietnam War ends.

September 25th – Declan Donnelly is born.

October 31st – Queen release their single *Bohemian Rhapsody*.

November 18th – Anthony McPartlin is born.

1976

January 21st – The first commercial flight of the supersonic airliner Concorde.

March 4th – The first stage of the Eldon Square Shopping Centre in Newcastle is opened.

March 16th – Harold Wilson announces his resignation as Prime Minister.

Brendan Foster.

April 1st – The Apple Computer Company is founded by Steve Jobs and Steve Wozniak.

April 3rd – The United Kingdom wins the Eurovision Song Contest with the song *Save Your Kisses for Me* sung by Brotherhood of Man.

April 5th – James Callaghan becomes Prime Minister.

April 26th – Carry On star Sid James dies on stage at the Sunderland Empire Theatre.

June to August – A heat wave causes the worst drought in the Britain for over 300 years.

July 26th – Brendan Foster wins the bronze medal in the 10,000 metres at the Montreal Olympic Games. It is Britain's only track and field medal at the games.

September 23rd – A fire on the destroyer HMS *Glasgow* while being fitted out at Swan Hunter's shipyard in Wallsend kills eight men.

November 2nd – Jimmy Carter wins the US Presidential election, defeating incumbent Gerald Ford.

November 26th – Punk group the Sex Pistols release their first single *Anarchy in the UK*.

1977

April 18th to 30th – The World Snooker Championship is played at the Crucible Theatre in Sheffield for the first time.

June 7th – Silver Jubilee public holiday to celebrate twenty-five years of the Queen's reign.

August 16th – Elvis Presley dies in his home in Graceland at the age of 42.

October 1st – Pele, while with New York Cosmos, plays his final professional football game.

November 15th – The first SavaCentre hypermarket in Britain is opened in Washington.

December 27th – *Star Wars* opens in British cinemas.

1978

April 2nd – TV show *Dallas* is shown on television for the first time in America.

May 1st – May Day becomes a Bank Holiday for the first time.

July 25th – The world's first test-tube baby, Louise Brown, is born in Oldham.

October 16th – John Paul II becomes Pope. He is the first non-Italian Pope for over 400 years.

Lord Mountbatten on a visit to South Tyneside in 1978.

1979

January 22nd – The biggest day of strike action in Britain since the General Strike of 1926. The winter of 1978/79 became known as the 'Winter of Discontent' with strikes by workers including petrol tanker and lorry drivers, hospital ancillary staff, ambulance men and dustmen.

February 9th – Trevor Francis becomes Britain's first £1 million footballer when he moves from Birmingham City to Nottingham Forest.

May 4th – The Conservatives win the General Election and Margaret Thatcher becomes the first female Prime Minister.

August 27th – Lord Mountbatten, the Queen's cousin, is assassinated by the IRA. A bomb planted on his yacht also kills three others.

December 11th – The closure of Consett Steelworks is announced.

A magazine produced during the campaign against the closure of Consett Steelworks.

Also available from Summerhill Books

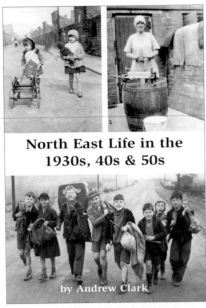

North East Life in the 1930s, 40s & 50s
by Andrew Clark

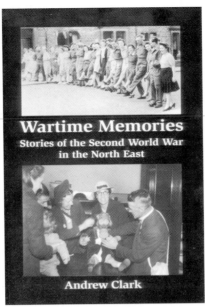

Wartime Memories
Stories of the Second World War in the North East
Andrew Clark

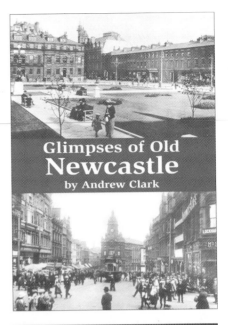

Glimpses of Old Newcastle
by Andrew Clark

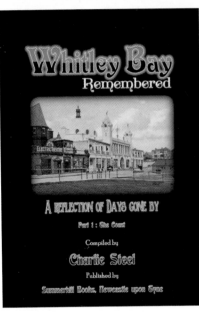

Whitley Bay Remembered
A Reflection of Days Gone By
Part 1 : The Coast
Compiled by Charlie Steel
Published by Summerhill Books, Newcastle upon Tyne

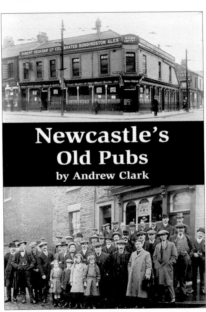

Newcastle's Old Pubs
by Andrew Clark

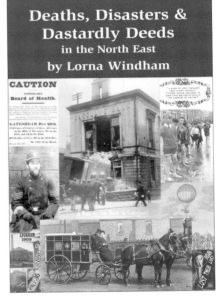

Deaths, Disasters & Dastardly Deeds
in the North East
by Lorna Windham

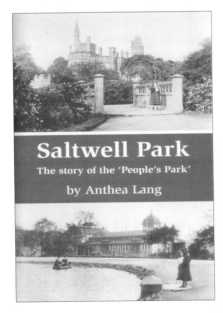

Saltwell Park
The story of the 'People's Park'
by Anthea Lang

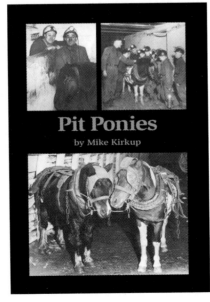

Pit Ponies
by Mike Kirkup

Memories of Gateshead
by Kathleen Harrison